Soap Making Like A Pro

The Complete Guide with Recipes on How to Make Colorful & Fragrant Soap at Home for Fun & Profit

Vanessa D. Langton

Copyright© 2015 by Vanessa D. Langton

Soap Making Like A Pro

Copyright© 2015 Vanessa D. Langton

All Rights Reserved.

Warning: The unauthorized reproduction or distribution of this copyrighted work is illegal. No part of this book may be scanned, uploaded or distributed via internet or other means, electronic or print without the author's permission. Criminal copyright infringement without monetary gain is investigated by the FBI and is punishable by up to 5 years in federal prison and a fine of $250,000. (http://www.fbi.gov/ipr/). Please purchase only authorized electronic or print editions and do not participate in or encourage the electronic piracy of copyrighted material.

Publisher: Living Plus Healthy Publishing

ISBN-13: 978-1506130224

ISBN-10: 1506130224

Disclaimer

The Publisher has strived to be as accurate and complete as possible in the creation of this book. While all attempts have been made to verify information provided in this publication, the Publisher assumes no responsibility for errors, omissions, or contrary interpretation of the subject matter herein. Any perceived slights of specific persons, peoples, or organizations are unintentional.

This book is not intended for use as a source of legal, business, accounting or financial advice. All readers are advised to seek services of competent professionals in the legal, business, accounting, and finance fields.

The information in this book is not intended or implied to be a substitute for professional medical advice, diagnosis or treatment. All content contained in this book is for general information purposes only. Always consult your healthcare provider before carrying on any health program.

Table of Contents

Chapter 1: Introduction to Soap Making 3

Chapter 2: History of Making Soap 9

Chapter 3: Ingredients for Soap Making 19

Chapter 4: Tools and Supplies for Soap Making 35

    Soap Molds 40

Chapter 5: Making Modern Soap 43

    Basic Cold Processing Method 45
    Tracing 47
    Recipes 48

Chapter 6: Unique Types of Soap & More Recipes 81

    Shampoo Recipes 101
    Laundry Detergent Recipes 109

Chapter 7: Starting a Soap Making Business 119

Chapter 8: Putting it All Together 127

Chapter 1: Introduction to Soap Making

The art of making soap is a complex one. True soap making is part craft and part chemistry. Fortunately, soap making doesn't end up with bars and bars of plain white soap. There are a great many types of soaps to be made of different colors, scents and purposes. In this guide, you will learn how soap was made throughout history and find ways to make your own soap so that you can potentially start your own soap making business.

Soap is a popular gift to give for birthdays, Christmas, bridal showers and Mother's day. You can also make it year round and sell it at boutiques and craft fairs. You may or may not make your money's worth if you are making soap just for your family. The idea is to have fun and make some soap people would enjoy.

Before getting into the details of making soap, we should talk about the science of soap making. Basically, soap is the salt of a fatty acid. Fatty acids are the base components of fats. Soap throughout the ages has been the sodium salt or the potassium salt of a fatty acid.

A salt is part of what happens when you mix an acid and an alkali together. Acids and alkalis don't really like each other so they split up to form salts. There are many possible salts out there besides the typical sodium chloride or table salt. An acid is a liquid with a pH of less than 7.0 and is something like vinegar or sulfuric acid. Alkali tends to corrode things, whereas acids burn things. An alkali has a pH of greater than 7.0. Sodium bicarbonate or baking soda is an alkali. Alkalis tend to be slippery to the touch.

A fatty acid, as mentioned is a building block of fat. They are contained in oils like vegetable oils, fish oils and animal fats. You need fatty acids to make the backbone of soap.

There are three separate steps to making the kind of soap that was made centuries ago until other chemical processes took over. These three steps include:

- Making wood ash lye.
- Cleaning the fat.
- Boiling the above two ingredients so they come together to make soap.

The first necessary item is a liquid solution of lye, also called potash. Wood ashes are placed in a barrel with no bottom that is set on a stone slab with a groove in it. Water is poured into the barrel until the brownish liquid comes out of the bottom of the barrel and travels along the groove until it drips into a clay vessel beneath it. This is your potash.

Then you clean the fats through the smelly process of rendering. This process removes any leftover meat pieces or food pieces left over from using cooking fat. Fat you get from beef cattle is called tallow and fat you get from pork is called lard.

You might imagine that fat left around for days on end (or longer) would get rancid. Well, it does. The soap you make with rancid grease would work as well but it wouldn't smell the same as when it is rendered. In rendering, you take the fats and waste grease from cooking and add an equal amount of water. Because of the smell, this is an outdoor process. The fat and water are boiled. The solution is covered and allowed to cool. The clean, rendered fat rises to the surface and forms a solid layer.

Now you can make the soap. If you use pearlash, you put the potash in a kiln to burn off the impurities so that the result is a solid, white powder.

Next, you put the "right amount" of lye into a pot with the right amount of fat. This is a tricky process. You boil the combination of chemicals for 6-8 hours to get soap. What you get after the boiling process is soft soap. It's a brown jelly that is slippery and mixed with water to create soapy water. If you want hard soap, you add salt into the boiling soap pot and the end result is a hard soap. In the days before salt became plentiful, most people just used soft soap because salt was too precious of a commodity to waste on making soap hard.

In the boiling kettle, the fat breaks down into fatty acids and the fatty acids mix with alkali in a process called *saponification*. The sodium or potassium part of the alkali goes to make soap by combining with the fatty acid.

Another thing that comes from the fat breakdown process is glycerin. Glycerin can be left in the soap or can be washed out to become a useful byproduct. If olive oil is used instead of animal fat to make soap, the result is a cleaner, nicer smelling product.

Technically, any fat can be used with an alkali to make a soapy substance. You can make Lithium salts with fatty acids and this process results in soap that is used to make greases. Other oils that can be used to make soaps are coconut oil, palm oil, and laurel oil—each of which has its own characteristics and feel. If olive oil is used, the end result is Castile or Marseille soap, which is considered to be a very mild soap.

As you can see, there are many different things you can do to make soap and this doesn't even begin to include recipes for soap that have herbs, colorants or things like oatmeal in it. This is what makes soap making so exciting—one you will hopefully have years of fun with.

Chapter 2: History of Making Soap

Soap, while not strictly a necessity, has been a nice thing to have around for centuries. The earliest known soap making materials were found at archaeological sites dating back to 2800 BCE out of early Babylon. Around 500 BCE, soap was made from ashes, cypress oil and sesame seed oil. It was apparently used by servants who washed clothing. Another recipe for soap was found on a clay tablet out of Babylon from 2200 BCE. It consisted of water, cassia oil and alkali.

Even before that, it was likely that prehistoric man came in contact with soap. They may have noticed that ashes and meat fats created a foamy substance or that a foamy substance was created in pots boiling meat with fat in it that also got ashes from the fire in it. They may have discovered that when they washed the pot afterward, the foam caused the pot to become cleaner and maybe their hands got cleaner. If they used soap regularly, we'll probably never know.

The Egyptians used soap for bathing and combined alkali salts and vegetable or animal oils and fats to make soap for washing. Soap was also used to wash the wool that was eventually used in the weaving process.

Soap in Ancient Rome was made from animal fat, called tall, and ashes. According to Pliny the Elder, it was primarily used by the Germans and Gauls and was not considered a positive thing to use. In Rome, soap was used to shape the hair into fashionable shapes. As early as 100 AD, the Gauls or Celts used a soap-like substance formed into balls. This was the first time the substance was referred to as soap. The Latin word for soap until then had been "sapo."

Interestingly, the Romans did not use soap for washing their body but instead used it to wash textiles, such as wool fibers before making into cloth. Soap was made out of goat tallow and wood ashes, with the addition of salt to make the soap harder. In Pompeii, at the time of 79 AD, an entire soap factory was discovered, complete with bars ready for sale.

Remember the Roman baths? They didn't use soap at these baths but instead washed themselves with sand and olive oil. A strigil or scraper was used to scrape off the dirt and dead skin cells until the skin was considered "clean." A gentle rubdown and the putting on of herbal salves completed the cleansing process.

For most of history, herbal baths were preferred over soap baths. Even the beautiful Cleopatra routinely bathed in mare's milk. By the First Century ACE, doctor's used soap to treat diseases. The famous physician, Galen, recommended using soap to treat various skin conditions. Using soap on the body for the average person didn't come to Rome for several more centuries.

Soap in solid form has not been discovered from sites or literature in Northern Europe until the 1200s. At that point, soap was imported from the Islamic parts of Spain and from Northern Africa. Soap in the Islamic communities was made in great quantities and exported to other parts of the world. The main ingredient was from ashes and consisted of alkali.

In Naples, Italy, soap making became one of the guilds with expert soap makers making soap for the rest of the community. This began in the late 500s ACE. Over the next 200 years, soap making was everywhere across Spain and Italy. The making of soap was felt to be the work of women, who worked as much as men did in the creation of products for the villages.

By the 1400s, the professional manufacturing of soap was present in a few areas of France; these were the areas that sold soap to the rest of the country. In England, the center of soap production was in London. By the 1500s in Europe, soap became more than just tallow and alkali. Products containing olive oil instead of tallow were made as "fancy soaps" and some of these soaps are still made today. Italy is famous for its "Castile soap"—a white soap created only from vegetable oils and alkalis.

Soap took on a great role in colonial times where it was made in small quantities, usually by women. Initially, the fine oils of Europe were unavailable to colonials so they used wood ashes and waste animal fats. The wood ash and fats were boiled along with water to make a fairly harsh and malodorous soap. The soap was made from potash and was therefore potassium-based. Soap from potash was essentially the only kind of soap made until the first part of the 1800s, when the LeBlanc method was used to make a sodium-based soap that was then made on an industrial level. The only other people believed to have been able to produce a sodium alkali-based soap were the ancient Egyptians and those in the 8th century Spain. Coastal areas that burned seaweed to get ashes also were unknowingly making sodium-based soap.

The very first settlers brought soap with them from England. One ship, called the Talbot, which was chartered for use by the Massachusetts Bay Colony, carried 2 firkins of soap for Boston and Salem. This amounted to about 18 gallons of soap in two barrels.

Most soap in colonial America was made from a combination of pearlash and potash. Both of these are potassium-based and are alkalis that come from burning wood and plant material. Soap making held a great deal of superstition over the centuries, with no one really understanding the chemistry of soap making. It became a trial and error procedure, with many superstitions abounding about how to make a good soap.

Early settlers kept their fire ashes and the fat from cattle or other animals and, once or twice a year, held events where people from the homesteads got together to make soap. Any tallow or waste cooking grease was put together to make soap.

Soap making was considered to be a very difficult job. One needed to know if the strength of the lye was correct. They did this in colonial America by floating an egg or potato in the lye. If it floated "right" then it was the right strength. About a quarter-sized section of an egg or potato must be above the lye for it to be perfect for making soap. Water or more ashes were added to make the lye weaker or stronger.

To make soap, peddlers would often travel from farm to village, paying cash for wood ashes. The wood ashes would then go to factories that converted the potash into pearlash using their kiln. There was also usually a stone building called an ashery, which was for the express purpose of burning wood into ash. Burnt wood from fires on the outside of an ashery was felt to contain too much alkali so indoor burning of wood was preferred. There was a small opening at the bottom of the ashery where ash was removed from the burning wood.

As people moved in toward the end of the 1700s, the wood was much scarcer. There was less potash and pearlash around. A few years later, the LeBlanc Method was invented and caustic soda was used instead of potash. Eventually, this led to the lack of a need for potash and pearlash.

The LeBlanc Method created sodium hydroxide, a strong lye. Salt was no longer required to make soap hard and the firm quality of the soap was preferred by customers. No longer were acres and acres of trees necessary to create the amount of ash necessary for the population's needs.

In larger, more populated areas, some people took up soap making as a profession. The soap maker would add salt to the soap so that it could be hardened. It was cooled in a large wooden crate or form and then people would buy what they needed by the pound by having chunks of the large "bar" chopped off. Some of the soaps were scented with herbal concoctions such as caraway, wintergreen and lavender. Bars that were made small and wrapped weren't on the market until the mid-1800s.

Those who chose soap making as a profession were called "Soapboilers". Because beef fat or tallow was also used to make candles, some men were both soapboilers and chandlers, making both soap and candles for a living. Soapboilers in the colonies were in existence as early as 1609 in Jamestown.

Both potash and pearlash were considered valuable for the colonies and were two things that could be directly traded to the English for cold, hard cash. Pearlash was more expensive than potash because pearlash was used also to make glass. These were two commodities the English wanted out of the colonists as part of the colonies being subordinate to the crown. Potash is the residue that could be gotten when lye has been leached from wood ashes. Pearlash is made by baking potash inside a kiln to get rid of its carbon impurities. The end result was a fine white powder.

By the 1800s, the process of making soap became a great deal easier. This made soap cheaper and more people took to the idea of bathing with soap. The making of soap was considered an art form and a craft during the Victorian era and, using sodium hydroxide, the making of soap became a much larger industry.

Today's "soap" is actually not soap in the true definition of the word. Today's soaps are detergents made from oil-based constituents. There are some "soap" products created from natural substances that are so changed by the process of making the soap that it really doesn't resemble traditional soap.

Chapter 3: Ingredients for Soap Making

To simply make soap, you need just two ingredients: alkali and oil or fat. Mix these two things together under the right conditions and you get saponification or the making of soap. But soap making is much more fun than that. There are scores of different oils to use and many more additives—all of which combine to make different types and uses for your soap.

For example, the oil you use can make a great deal of difference in the kind of soap you get. The following is a table that can show you the different types of oils you can use as part of the ingredients you put in any given batch of soap:

	Hard/Soft	Cleansing	Fluffy Lather	Stable Lather	Skin Care
Avocado Oil	Soft	Fair	Yes	No	Excellent
Castor Oil	Soft	Fair	Yes	Yes	Great
Coconut Oil	Hard	Great	Yes	No	Fair
Olive Oil	Soft	Good	No	No	Great
Soybean Oil	Soft	Good	No	Yes	Fair
Palm Oil	Hard	Great	No	Yes	Fair
Sweet Almond Oil	Soft	Good	No	Yes	Excellent
Peanut Oil	Soft	Fair	No	Yes	Great
Jojoba Oil	Soft	Fair	No	Yes	Great
Kukui Oil	Soft	Good	No	Yes	Great
Tallow	Hard	Good	No	Yes	Fair
Lard	Hard	Good	No	Yes	Fair

You don't have to use only one kind of oil as you'll see in the following recipes. You can use combinations of oil to create different textures and properties of soap. Let's look at a couple of recipes just to give you an idea of the ingredients you might need. We will discuss more on tools you will need and the procedures of making soap in the next 2 chapters.

Basic Soap

Ingredients:

- 1.3 oz of castor oil
- 6.5 oz of coconut oil
- 6.5 oz of palm oil
- 3.1 oz of lye
- 7.5 oz of olive oil
- 1 oz of essential oil fragrance
- 8 oz of water

Directions:

1. Mix the lye solution. It will be hot so you need to set it aside to cool. Heat solid oils until they have melted and then add the liquid oils.

2. Bring the oil and lye temperatures to about 100-110 degrees Fahrenheit.

3. Slowly add the lye to the oils and stir with a stick blender.

4. Mix the soap by alternating short blasts with the blender and stirring with the stick.

5. Add the fragrance oil when the soap begins to form.

6. Put raw soap into mold and let it set for at least 12-24 hours.

7. Slice it into bars and cure it for another two to four weeks.

Soap with Olive Oil and Tallow

Ingredients:
- 4.2 oz of lye
- 9.6 oz of olive oil
- 22.4 oz of beef tallow
- 1.4 oz of essential oil
- 10.5 oz of water

Directions:

1. Mix the lye and allow it to cool.

2. Measure and melt tallow. When the tallow is melted, add the olive oil.

3. When both parts of the soap are at 100-110 degrees Fahrenheit, stir with a stick blend-

er, using short blasts of the blender intermixed with stirring.

4. Add essential oil.

5. Pour melted soap into mold.

6. Let it sit for about 12-24 hours or until it has completely cooled and is hard enough to slice into blocks.

7. Let the blocks cure for about two to four weeks.

You need to have some kind of oil or fat and lye. Those things can be purchased at supply stores for candle making. You also need something to make your soap smell good and possibly some kind of colorant.

If you're making soap with natural ingredients in them, there are many to choose from. There are some natural ingredients you can add to soap to make the soap more exfoliating or to have some other special properties. You can add flower petals, spices, and many types of herbs. Additives can add texture to the soap or can change the color of the soap. Some people infuse the soap with tea instead of using water.

Try to use organically grown herbs and spices, those that don't have any pesticides or other chemicals in them. You can even try growing your own additives in the garden. Most soap suppliers will sell spices, herbs and flower petals. Fresh herbs are better for soap than dried herbs and check the products you use for having a good color and odor

Additives you might try:

- **Basil**. This is an herb with a great deal of folklore behind it. Use crushed, dried basil leaves in the soap to create a speckled greenish-brown color.

- **Alkanet**. This is an herb that acts as a colorant to your soap. The colors you can get include purple, blue, red and pink. Its color changes with the pH so, depending on the pH of the end result, your color will be different. The more fatty acids you have or the more citric acid you have in your bath bombs, the redder your color will be. Slightly alkaline soap will be a bluish mauve color. It is a good herb to use with a tea infusion.

- **Calendula Petals**. Calendula is an old English marigold with an amazing sunshine orange color. It was felt to represent love in the medieval era. You need to crush the petals and expect that your soap will turn a beautiful orange color with slow fading potential. This flower allows your soap to have many healing properties related to the skin.

- **Bladderwrack**. This is a lightly scented seaweed product that gives your soap a lovely greenish color. Crush the bladder wrack before putting it into the soap. While it can feel coarse when you touch it, it instantly softens upon contact with the water.

- **Cayenne pepper**. This makes your soap have a light salmon color and doesn't fade really quickly. Put a teaspoon in a batch of soap and the soap will turn into a baby pink color. Add more to get a deeper coloration.

- **Cardamom**. This is a native Asian herb that delivers a spicy, warm scent to your soap. Put the finely ground herb in your soap in order to energize and uplift yourself. It also potentially enhances your circulation.

- **Cinnamon**. When put in soap, cinnamon gives the bar a warm, speckled brown color. You can use it in other bath, body and spa products as well. It delivers a spicy, warm scent and is believed to help you reduce stress. It stimulates you and acts as an astringent in your bath. You can imbed a curled part of cinnamon bark to decorate your bars of soap.

- **Chamomile Tea**. When infused into your soap it lightly colors it and you will notice a delightful herb-like fragrance.

- **Cloves**. This is a strongly scented herb with a spicy scent you won't be able to forget. If you use them in ground form, your soap bars will be a warm brown color. It's perfect when used as soap for the holidays. Be aware, though, that some people are sensitive to clove when it is used in soap on the skin.

- **Citrus Peel**. Try putting finely grated citrus peels into your soap because they add cute little specks of color to the end product. You can use citrus slices as a "garnish" on the top of the soap bars. They give off a bright citrus scent and impart an astringent quality to the soap. Make sure you put the peel in the soap just before pouring the raw soap into the mold because the citrus peels can inhibit tracing of the soap.

- **Green Tea**. This can be infused into the soap. The coloration is slight but the tea imparts antioxidant properties to the soap. Green tea also contains flavonoids and indoles, which are healthy for you.

- **Frankincense**. This is a unique herb that can be added whole or ground to change the coloration and scent of the soap.

- **Juniper berry**. These can be added to holiday soaps or any time that you want to provide texture and a rich coloration to the soap.

- **Indigo**. This is an Indian shrub that is fermented so that it provides a strong blue dye. Just a few grains of indigo impart a strong color to natural soaps and other bath products. Put only a small amount in the mixture or you will get a bluish discoloration to your skin.

- **Loofa**. This comes from the ocean and is a great natural exfoliator. Pour your raw soap into pieces of Loofa and the soap will be interspersed among the elements of Loofa. Loofa cylinders make especially good gifts.

- **Lavender Buds**. These have been in use since the ancient Romans used them as deodorants. They provide for a relaxing and healing bath with an aromatic flair. The buds are an azure bluish color and, whether they are ground or whole, the bars are beautiful. You can even "garnish" your bar with a small collection of buds.

- **Nettle leaves**. These are also called stinging nettles. They are great when put in shampoos because the nettle leaves get rid of dandruff. It is also said to reduce hair loss. Use them in natural soap shampoo bars and, besides a nice smell, you'll get a lovely green coloration to your soap.

- **Myrrh**. This is a lot like frankincense; however, its color is darker. If you put a bit of myrrh powder to the raw soap you can get a warm, pinkish brown coloration to your soap.

- **Parsley**. This is an herb that works well as a tea infusion or mixed as powdered, dried leaves. The color of the soap will be a light apple green color that unfortunately fades rather quickly. To preserve the color of the soap, store the soap out of the sunshine.

- **Paprika**. This spice imparts a beautiful rich, red color when added to handmade soaps. If you're using paprika in bath bombs, use only a little bit or you'll get a red ring around the tub.

- **Rose buds, Rose Petals, Rose Hips**. These can be used as a "garnish" for soap bars and when added to raw soap, you get a nice speckled look to the soaps. Rose buds act as a gentle exfoliants, which will nicely cleanse your skin. If you grind the rose petals, your soap will be a nice pinkish brown color.

- **Poppy seeds**. You can use blue or white poppy seeds, which will nicely speckle the handmade soaps. These are a great gentle cleansers and exfoliants that are used in many types of soaps.

- **Rosemary**. Take the leaves of this herb and crush it into a powder. It is a mossy green colorant to soap and body products. It acts as an antiseptic and makes a fine hair tonic which will make your hair shiny. You can make a rosemary tea and infuse it into hair rinse solutions and handmade shampoo bars. You can use dried, whole rosemary to improve your circulation. It also has a great scent.

- **Rose Geranium**. You can turn this herb into chopped or powdered leaves that add a lovely green color to your soaps. The color fades over time to a yellowish green color. You can't use pot geranium; instead use the highly scented geranium leaves.

- **Safflower**. This herb is also called face saffron even though it isn't related to saffron. The petals you use are in deep reddish orange that look nice in homemade soaps without a great deal of fading. You can mix the safflower soap with talcum powder, which turns the soap the color of blush or rouge.

- **Spirulina seaweed**. It has the lovely smell of the ocean beach but this aroma fades over time. You can cover up the scent with an essential oil if you don't like it. It produces a very rich green coloration to the soap which fades over time to an earthy green color. You can use this product in teas, scrubs, bath salts and bath powders.

- **Soapwort**. This is an herb that has multiple, nicely scented, delicate flowers and oval leaves. The roots, stems and leaves of this plant contain a natural form of saponins, which makes a nice shampoo after boiling. It's possible to put dried leaves and roots in your soap as well.

- **Turmeric**. Like indigo, you can't use turmeric in massage melts because it will stain your hands. Used correctly, it makes soap a lovely peachy color.

- **Thyme**. Thyme has lovely small green leaves that can add texture to soap or other bath products.

- **Wheat germ**. This is an exfoliant perfect for bar soap. It is also great for those with sensitive skin as it is soothing and softening. You can also use wheat germ in other bath and spa products.

- **Walnut leaves**. Use these leaves in powdered form to make for a rich, dark greenish brown coloration. Use crushed instead of powdered leaves for a speckled look.

- **Witch Hazel**. You can use the leaves or the extract of witch hazel to act as an astringent in your soap. It also adds some color and aroma.

As you can see, the variety of soaps you can make are practically endless. You can make regular bar soap with exfoliants in them or a nice bath bomb with paprika in them. Because of this variety, you can create as many types of soap as you can think of.

Chapter 4: Tools and Supplies for Soap Making

Fortunately, with the making of soap today, you won't likely have to render fat over an open fire outside, nor will you have to make potash out of a year's supply of wood ashes. You will, however, need to gather some tools and equipment in order to make soap for pleasure or profit.

There are several methods for making soap that rely on slightly different pieces of equipment. For example, there is the cold press method, which is used most commonly by those who make soap at home. The process of neutralization happens as the process is molding. There is the semi-boiled method, in which the heat is applied using a double boiler. This neutralizes the soap prior to being molded. There is the full-boiled method in which you prepare all the ingredients together in a single container. Then heat is added, causing the soap to neutralize. This is how glycerin is made.

If you are making transparent soap, you need to add solvents like alcohol to prevent crystals from developing while the soap is cooling. This is called "glycerin soap". This kind of soap is good for oily skin as it is known to dry out the skin. You can also take glycerin in its most pure form and solidify it with the use of plasticizer chemicals. You can also create a foamy glycerin by adding detergents. Most of these types of soaps are made synthetically.

Items you'll need (in general) to create the soap include:

- At least **one stainless steel bowl**. Choose a big bowl that will catch all the splatter as you are mixing the ingredients.

- You'll need a **Pyrex glass container** that is heat resistant and that holds at least two cups of liquid. This is where you will mix the lye and water. Too large a container and the heat will be lost too quickly and they won't be the right temperature for mixing with the oils and fats.

- It will get very hot so you'll need some **heating pads** for your hands as you manipulate the hot ingredients.

- You'll need a **stainless steel pot** in order to heat the oils in. Not all oils are liquid at room temperature so you'll need to heat them. You can also use a sturdy **microwave dish** to melt the oils.

- You'll need two **candy thermometers**, one for the lye and one for the oils. It's better to have two so you don't mix small amounts of oil into the lye prematurely or you could get splatter.

- You'll need a **heat source**, such as a hot plate, stove or microwave. These can be used to melt the fats and oils.

- **Protective wear** is also good including a long sleeved shirt, long pants and shoes. You'll need rubber gloves and chemistry goggles or glasses. This is a chemical reaction happening and just about anything can happen if you don't do it perfectly.

- **Soap Molds**. These can be made from plastic and be decorative or made of cardboard or wood, lined with waxed paper.

- **Measuring spoons** or a **Pyrex graduated cylinder** that can measure liquids carefully. Some ingredients are measured to the tenth of an ounce. If you get a graduated cylinder, the measurements will likely be in milliliters so you'll need to calculate the amount given the amount in ounces.

One milliliter = 0.033814 US fluid ounces

That means that 100 milliliters = 3.34 US fluid ounces. It also means you'll need a larger graduated cylinder that holds at least 300 milliliters for most recipes. If you use measuring cups, this means that 1 cup = 8 fluid ounces and 1 pint = 16 fluid ounces. Note that most oils and butters are actually weighed out.

- You'll need a **digital scale** that is accurate to at least 2 grams. This is because some ingredients are measured in grams instead of fluid ounces or milliliters.

- You'll need some **sticks** for blending the soap during the chemical reaction.

- You will want a **stick blender**. This is a blender that you hold in your hand and stick the blending part down into the ingredients. It is generally pulsed several times in between stirring it to make the soap.

- **Pipettes** are good for introducing liquid items in your soap mixture.

- A set of **measuring spoons** can help you measure out ingredients such as spices and herbs.

- A **knife** is necessary for cutting the soap into bars after the soap cools. It should be a fairly sharp knife.

- You should have **items for packaging** your soap such as rice paper or other kind of paper for wrapping and different mechanisms for tying your soap in its wrapper. You can also use stickers labeled with your company name, logo, and the name of the soap on your wrapped soap.

- **Safety goggles** and **rubber gloves** are a good idea whenever you're working around lye products.

- **Blankets** are used to cover molds after they have been poured so that the soap cools very slowly.

- **Freezer paper** is used to line the molds for easy release after they have cooled.

Soap Molds

Soap molds are best made from plastic, wood or cardboard. Do not use products made from aluminum, tin, copper or Teflon because these things interact with the lye and the soap may not turn out properly. Sometimes candle molds and candy molds work well, too.

For simple bars, make a wooden or cardboard mold that makes up to 20 bars of soap. After the soap cools, you can cut the soap into its separate bars. You can also use cardboard juice or milk containers because they are coated with wax and the soap doesn't stick. Recycled plastic bottles can be used to solidify soap before cutting.

If the soap doesn't break loose from the mold, go ahead and put the molded soap into the freezer for a couple of hours. The soap mixture will shrink a little bit and you'll be able to release it from the colder mold. You can also grease your molds with vegetable oil or use waxed paper to line cardboard or wooden molds. Treat your molds well and they will last a very long time.

Another tip is to use butcher's paper or brown freezer paper to line the molds. Start with vegetable oil and lay down the freezer paper with the shiny side toward the soap. After you remove the soap from the mold you can peel off the paper from the soap and cut the soap.

Chapter 5: Making Modern Soap

Making modern soap isn't so very different from making soap in the old days. You have to mix fat or oil with something alkali. In the colonial times, the fat was lard or tallow, made from animal fats. The alkali was potash or a purified form of potash called pearlash. Soap was made hard using ordinary table salt.

Today's soap making involves using sodium hydroxide lye, which already contains the sodium to make the soap hard. The biggest difference is in the type of fat used. Now multiple types of plant oils are used instead of animal fats in many cases so the soap is mild and healthy for you. Some plant oils make only soft soaps while others make hard soaps.

In this chapter, we will look into how to make simple modern bar soaps. In the chapter after this, we will talk about making fancy soaps and other bath products made from soap. First some simple tips:

- When making beeswax soaps, use separate utensils. The reason for this is that beeswax doesn't come off the utensils easily. The higher melting temperature of beeswax can create a fire hazard and can damage the other oils you are using. Add essential oils when the soap is cooling so as to avoid boiling off the essential oil. If the resultant mixture is too thin, add more beeswax.

- If you have a nice, expensive scale, cover it in a clear, cheap inexpensive plastic bag so that spills get on the bag. You can change the bag out to a different bag every so often when the existing bag gets dirty enough.

- Clean the soap out of containers and molds by microwaving them for a little bit. The components melt a bit and you can wash them out more easily. Hand-wash your dishes with liquid dishwashing soap. You can also use green scrubbing pads to scrub out the materials.

- When you get good at soap making, you can do your soap making reaction by feel. This means that you can judge when the temperature of the soap is about equal and around 100 degrees and then mix them.

- Some practitioners of the trade mix the oils and butters in hot lye, allowing the lye to melt the solid oils. The end result is a solution that is the right temperature and can then be blended.

- Use your goat milk, juice, pumpkin juice and distilled water frozen. You can put your lye in with these solutions and the lye doesn't get as hot and reaches its proper temperature without so much waiting.

- Use a coffee grinder to grind herbs and spices, cleaning it out every time you're switching recipes.

Basic Cold Processing Method

Always wear goggles and rubber gloves. Weigh out lye into a plastic container and weigh out water or other liquid. Pour the lye into the water in a well-ventilated area. Avoid splashing. The mixture will be hot so you'll need to set it aside to cool with a thermometer in it. When the lye reaches 100-125 degrees, it will be ready to mix with the oils. Since this can take several hours, you'll need to put it in a cold water or ice bath to cool faster.

Weigh out your butters and oils and put them into a pot. Allow them to reach between 100-125 degrees. Both the lye and oils must be about the same temperature. You can prepare your additives in the meantime. Weigh or measure out some herbs if you're adding herbs to your soap. If you're using a solid pigment, mix it in a small amount of glycerin before adding to the soap mixture.

Line your mold container with freezer paper so it lets loose easier after cooling. Set this aside for when your soap is made.

When oils and lye are the same temperature between 100 and 125 degrees, add the lye to the oils slowly, continually stirring. You can use a spoon or a stick blender. When the soap reaches trace (see below for definition), you can add your additives and blend in well.

Pour your soap into its mold and cover with freezer paper and a piece of cardboard. Put your mold into blankets so that it slowly cools down over 24-48 hours. Unmold the soap and cut into blocks immediately. Place bars on a drying rack or open box until it is cured for at least 2-3 weeks. The longer it cures, the harder and milder the soap will be.

Tracing

Before you begin making soap, you need to understand the process of "tracing". This is where the magic happens and you reach the point of no return in the soap making process. When your soap traces, it will not go back into oil and lye.

To test for tracing, you dip a spatula or a spoon into the mixture. Then dribble a little bit of it back into the pot. If it leaves a "trace" of soap behind, the soap has traced. It looks just like a small mound or so of soap left on the spoon. In addition to trace, there should be no more streaks of leftover oil in the mixture. You can pour your soap after seeing a light "trace" with a little bit of soap on the spoon, or a heavy trace, with a big lump of soap left on the spoon.

Recipes

Now let's make some soap. Most ingredients listed below are measured out by weight rather than volume.

Basic Soap Recipe

Ingredients:

- 5.5 ounces of castor oil
- 16 ounces of coconut oil
- 40 ounces of olive oil
- 30 ounces of hydrogenated soy oil
- 12.5 ounces lye
- 5.5 tsp salt
- 5.5 tsp sugar
- 34 fl ounces of distilled water

Directions:

1. Mix the lye with 30 fluid ounces of water.

2. Place the salt and sugar into the remaining 4 ounces of water and add this back to the lye solution.

3. Let the lye cool down to 125 degrees.

4. Warm all the oils until they reach 125 degrees and blend until soap is made (the trace needs to be made).

5. Pour soap into molds. One interesting mold is a cut through 2-4 inch PVC pipe sealed at both ends with tape.

6. Unmold the soap and cut into bars.

Oil and Tallow-Based Soap

Ingredients:

- 12 ounces of lye
- 28 ounces cold water
- 4 ounces of olive oil
- 52 ounces of canola oil
- 9 ounces of castor oil
- 30 ounces of tallow (you can also use Crisco or lard)
- Fragrance
- Colorant

Directions:

1. Mix lye and water in a glass, enamel or plastic container.

2. Let this mixture sit until the product is 95 degrees.

3. In the meantime, heat the oils and tallow until the combination is about 110 degrees.

4. Put additives into the warm oil mixture.

5. Add lye to the oil solution and blend or stir until the soap has a light trace.

6. Pour into molds greased with mineral oil. Let it sit for 12-24 hours.

7. Cut into bars and cure for an additional two weeks.

Emollient Soap

Ingredients:
- 4.5 ounces lye
- 1.9 ounces of illipe butter (Shorea stenoptera seed butter)
- 6.4 ounces of palm kernel oil
- 6.4 ounces of coconut oil
- 3.2 ounces of palm oil
- 4.8 ounces of kokum butter
- 3.8 ounces of mango butter

- 3.2 ounces of shea butter
- 2.2 ounces of lanolin
- 11.5 ounces water
- 1 ounce pear berry fragrance
- Super-fat the product with 1.1 ounces of meadow foam and 1.1 ounces of avocado oil

Directions:

1. Mix lye and water and allow it to cool to 90 degrees.

2. Warm fat and all oils over low to medium heat until it melts.

3. Pour lye solution into oils when both are 80-90 degrees. Stir or blend until it reaches a light trace.

4. Add avocado oil and the meadow foam at the end and continue to stir to a medium trace.

5. Pour into molds and let solidify over 24 hours.

6. Cure the bars or molded items for 3-4 weeks. This makes about 2 pounds of soap

or about 6-8 bars, depending on the size and shape of your mold.

Azuki Bean Exfoliant Soap

This is a lovely exfoliant type of soap that will also moisturize your skin.

Ingredients:

- 2.83 ounces of lye
- Ground Azuki beans sold in Asian grocery stores—1/2 cup
- 4 ounces Neroli Hydrosol
- 4 ounces of cucumber floral water
- Few Chamomile leaves
- 4 ounces of olive oil
- 1 ounce of sunflower oil
- 3 ounces of castor oil
- 6 ounces of coconut oil
- 4 ounces of palm oil
- Basil fragrance oil
- Mandarin Orange Essential Oil
- 2 ounces of Kokum butter
- Vitamin E T50 as a preservative
- Green mica as a colorant

Directions:

1. Melt coconut oil and kokum butter.

2. Add the rest of the oils. Add lye to the floral waters. Make sure to have the temperature of both parts to be around 105 degrees.

3. Blend or stir by hand.

4. When it begins to thicken, add half of the azuki beans and a tablespoon of orange essential oil. Mix again and then add chamomile leaves and vitamin E.

5. When it looks like pea soup, add the rest of the azuki beans and pour into the mold.

6. Line mold with parchment paper and wrap soap and mold in towel so it cools slowly over a day or two.

7. Slice into bars.

Bay Rum Soap

Ingredients:

- 5.28 ounces of lye at 95 percent (5 percent discount)
- 6 ounces of palm kernel flakes
- 1 ounce of rice bran oil
- 6 ounces of Sesame seed oil
- 10 ounces of tallow
- 2 ounces of castor oil
- 6 ounces of coconut oil
- 6 ounces of olive oil
- 14 ounces of water (or half water and half Goat's milk)
- 5.28 ounces of water
- 1/2 to 1 ounce of Bay Rum fragrance oil

Directions:

1. Mix lye with water and/or goat's milk.

2. Melt all oils and palm kernel flakes. Keep temperatures at or below 90 degrees.

3. Use stick blender to stir. Watch closely as once this gets to a light trace it goes quickly.

4. Add fragrance oil at a light trace and then pour into molds.

5. Let cool over 24 hours and cure for 2-3 weeks.

Three Oil Soap

Ingredients:

- 4.3 ounces of lye
- 11.9 ounces of water
- 5.3 ounces of palm oil
- 21.8 ounces of olive oil
- 5.3 ounces of coconut oil
- 4 tsp fragrance oil of your choice
- 1 tsp ground chamomile

This makes three pounds of soap.

Directions:

1. Add lye to water and allow to cool.

2. Weigh out fats and melt to about 110-130 degrees Fahrenheit.

3. When temperature of lye also approaches 110-130 degrees, pour the lye into the fat

and stir until the mixture reaches a light trace, about 45-55 minutes.

4. Add herbs and fragrance oils just prior to pouring into molds.

5. Cover the top with saran wrap to avoid getting a powdery buildup. Wrap blankets around the mold so it cools slowly.

6. After 1-2 days, cut into bars and put wax paper above and below the bars.

7. Every few days, turn bars a quarter turn to cure evenly.

8. After two weeks, wrap the bars and let them cure an additional 2 weeks.

Honey Carrot Soap

Ingredients:

- 4.5 ounces of lye
- 13 ounces of fresh carrot juice (from a blender or juicer)
- 16 ounces vegetable shortening
- 4 ounces of sunflower oil
- 8 ounces of coconut oil

- 4 ounces of cocoa butter
- 2 tablespoons of honey
- 1/4 teaspoon of aloe vera fragrance oil
- 2 tablespoons of cucumber fragrance oil

Directions:

1. Mix lye with partially frozen (slushy) carrot juice. Let it cool to 110 degrees Fahrenheit.

2. Melt oils and butters until they reach the same temperature.

3. Use a stick blender and stir the lye and oil mixture, pulsing in one minute intervals until the mixture reaches trace.

4. Add honey and fragrance oils. Stir until blended. Pour into molds.

5. Cut into bars after 48 hours. Allow to cure for another 6 weeks before packaging.

Shampoo Bar

This is a bar soap that can be lathered on the head to wash the hair.

Ingredients:

- 17.95 ounces of lye (5 percent excess fat)
- 46 ounces water
- 32 ounces of olive oil
- 8 ounces of canola oil
- 24 ounces of palm oil
- 32 ounces of coconut oil
- 24 ounces of castor oil
- 8 ounces of sweet almond Oil
- Essential oils to create a scent

Directions:

1. Add lye to water and allow it to cool to 110 degrees.

2. Heat oils together to 110 degrees.

3. Add lye to oils and stir with stick blender until the mixture reaches trace.

4. Add scent and pour the batch into mold.

Milk Based Soap

Ingredients:

- 1/4 cup Red Devil lye granules
- 1/4 cup water
- 1/2 cup palm oil
- 1/2 cup coconut oil
- 1 cup vegetable shortening (Crisco)
- 1 cup milk or cream
- 1.5 teaspoons essential oil of your choice

Directions:

1. Add lye to water and milk or cream. Let it cool to 110-120 degrees

2. Melt shortening and add oils until they reach 110-120 degrees.

3. Add lye to oils and stir with stick blender until the mixture reaches trace, about 20 minutes.

4. Add essential oil when the soap traces.

5. Pour soap into mold and let sit for 2 days.

6. When it is removed from mold, cut the bars and let them cure for 3 weeks.

Tea Soap

Ingredients:

- 5.2 ounces of lye
- 12 ounces of water
- 8 ounces of olive oil
- 8 ounces of soybean oil
- 8 ounces of fractionated coconut oil
- 1/2 cup finely chopped cucumber
- 4 ounces unsalted butter
- 4 ounces of shea butter
- 4 ounces of aloe butter
- 1 tsp of chamomile essential oil
- 3 tazo tea bags (chamomile or green tea)

Directions:

1. Brew tea with boiling water and allow to seep in refrigerator until cold.

2. Squeeze out as much liquid as possible and save tea bags.

3. Puree the cucumber and add the contents of the used tea bags, a teaspoon of chamomile essential oil, and 1/3 teaspoon of liquapar or other preservative. Mix this together.

4. Melt shea butter until reaching 175 degrees, about 20 minutes.

5. Turn low heat and add the remaining butters and oils.

6. Put 12 ounces of cold brewed tea in a pot and add the lye.

7. Allow both mixtures to reach 100 degrees and add oil to lye mixture.

8. Put the entire pot into an ice water bath. Mix with a stick blender until it reaches a heavy trace.

9. Add cucumber puree and mix gently.

10. Pour into mold and let it rest for 2 days.

11. Cut the soap into bars and let cure for 3 weeks.

English Countryside Soap

Ingredients:

- 9 ounces of lye
- 24 ounces of water
- 4.3 ounces of castor oil
- 20 ounces of coconut oil
- 4.1 ounces of aloe oil
- 17.5 ounces of palm oil
- 11.4 ounces of canola oil
- 0.8 ounces of shea butter
- 0.8 ounces of cocoa butter
- 5.1 ounces of sweet almond oil
- 1.5 teaspoons of Neroli fragrance oil
- 1.5 teaspoons of Clove bud essential oil
- 1.5 teaspoons of spearmint essential oil
- 1/2 cup Calendula Petals put in at trace

Directions:

1. Blend fragrance oil and essential oils together 24 hours in advance and cover them.

2. Add lye to water and let it cool to 90-110 degrees.

3. Melt solid oils and heat liquid oils altogether until they reach 90-110 degrees.

4. Add lye solution to oils and stir with stick blender until it reaches trace.

5. Add essential/fragrance oils and calendula petals.

6. Mold and let sit for 1-2 days.

7. Cut into bars and let cure for another 2 weeks.

Castile Soap II

Ingredients:
- 4 ounces of lye
- 10 ounces of distilled water
- 21 ounces of pure olive oil
- 2 ounces of chamomile fragrance oil
- 1 ounce of beeswax pearls
- 1/4 cup chamomile, ground

Directions:

1. Add lye to the water, mixing it well and let it cool until it reaches 120 degrees.

2. Melt the beeswax and add olive oil until the mixture reaches 120 degrees.

3. Add the lye to the beeswax and oil mixture and stir until it reaches trace.

4. Add ground chamomile and chamomile oil to the traced mixture.

5. Pour into mold. Let it set for 2 days.

6. Cut into bars. Allow to cure for an additional 2 weeks.

Banana Soap

Ingredients:

- 4 ounces of lye
- 0.4 ounces of melted beeswax
- 9.2 ounces palm oil
- 1 ounce of olive oil
- 7.8 ounces coconut oil
- 0.6 ounces of apricot oil
- 5.3 ounces of sunflower oil
- 5.3 ounces of soybean oil
- 0.5 ounces of sweet almond oil
- 2 tbsp dried milk
- 7-8 ounces of crushed frozen milk

- 1.8 ounces of melted shea butter
- 1 frozen banana, mashed
- 1 tbsp banana fragrance oil

Directions:

1. Add lye to frozen milk. Heat oils to 150 degrees.

2. When oils and lye mixture have reached 110 degrees, add lye to oils and stir with stick blender until trace.

3. At trace, add the rest of the ingredients and stir.

4. Pour into mold. Allow to cool over 2 days.

5. Cut into bars. Allow to cure for another 2-3 weeks.

Mango Soap

Ingredients:

- 6.8 ounces lye
- 17 ounces water
- 16 ounces olive oil
- 16 ounces coconut oil
- 8 ounces shea butter
- 8 ounces mango butter
- 2 ounces fragrance of your choice (think tropical)

Directions:

1. Mix lye with water and allow it to reach a temperature of about 120 degrees.

2. Melt all butters and oils until they reach a temperature of 120 degrees.

3. Add lye to oil mixture and stir until the soap reaches a medium trace, add fragrance and stir it in.

4. Pour into mold and let cool over 1-2 days.

5. Cut into bars and allow it to cure for an additional 2 weeks.

Men's Beard Soap

Ingredients:

- 9.2 ounces of lye
- 24.4 ounces of frozen chopped Goat's milk
- 22.4 ounces of coconut oil
- 19.2 ounces of olive oil
- 9.6 ounces of palm oil
- 12.8 ounces of castor oil
- 2-3 ounces of essential oil of your choice
- Vulcanus Color Clay
- 1 ounce grapefruit seed extract
- Bay Rum for scenting

Directions:

1. Weigh out goat's milk and add lye to it a little at a time. Allow it to reach 100-125 degrees through cooling.

2. Melt oils until they reach 100-125 degrees.

3. Use a stick blender to mix lye mixture and oil mixture until it reaches trace.

4. Add essential oil, grapefruit extract, Vulcanus color clay, and bay rum scent.

5. When completely mixed, pour into mold and let it cool for 18-24 hours. Then put into freezer to let bars release.

6. Cut into bars and allow it to cure for an additional 4 weeks.

Hemp Soap

Hemp seed oil is especially good for the skin and is easily absorbed by skin cells. It contains Omega 3 and Omega 6 fatty acids. These provide a good anti-inflammatory power with anti-aging and moisture balancing abilities.

Ingredients:

- 13 ounces of lye
- 30 ounces of distilled water
- 27 ounces of coconut Oil
- 2 tsp of coral mica powder
- 10 drops of Vitamin E oil
- 32 ounces of palm Oil
- 15 ounces of olive Oil
- 16 ounces of Hemp Oil
- 4 ounces of Bergamot oil, Patchouli oil, and Lime oil Blend

Directions:

1. Mix lye with water and allow it to cool to 110 degrees.

2. Mix oils together and allow them to reach 110 degrees.

3. Add lye to oil mixture and stir with stick blender until it reaches trace.

4. Add fragrance oils and coral mica powder.

5. Mix thoroughly and pour into mold. Allow it to cure for 1-2 days.

6. Cut into bars. Allow the bars to cure for an additional 2 weeks.

Peppermint Soap

Ingredients:

- 2 ounces of lye
- 1 cup distilled water
- 1 ounce olive oil
- 4 ounces coconut oil
- 10 ounces of palm oil
- 1 ounce olive oil for cocoa powder
- 3 tablespoons cocoa powder
- 0.25 ounces of peppermint essential oil

Directions:

1. Mix lye with water and set aside to cool to 100 degrees.

2. Melt oils in same pot and when they reach 110 degrees,

3. Add lye with oils and stir with stick blender until it reaches trace.

4. Mix 1 ounce of olive oil with cocoa powder and add to soap along with peppermint essential oil. Stir well and pour into mold.

5. Cover with freezer paper or plastic wrap and wrap in blankets to allow cool slowly for 2 days.

6. Cut into bars. Allow soap to cure for an additional 2-3 weeks.

Lavender Soap

Ingredients:
- 1.25 ounces of lye
- 2.5 ounces of lavender-infused water
- 1 ounce of half and half
- 2.5 ounces of coconut oil
- 1.5 ounces of palm oil
- 4 ounces of olive oil
- 0.25 tsp of freesia fragrance oil
- 0.25 fluid ounces lavender essential oil

Directions:

1. Put lye in lavender water and then add half and half.

2. Melt oils to about 110 degrees.

3. When both mixtures are about the same temperature, mix lye slowly with oils, stirring constantly.

4. When the soap reaches trace, add lavender essential oil and freesia fragrance oil. Stir in carefully and then pour soap into mold.

5. Allow to cool in blankets for 24 hours.

6. Cut into bars. Allow soap to cure for an additional 2 weeks.

Beer Soap

Ingredients:

- 8.5 ounces of lye
- 22 ounces of extremely flat beer
- 4 ounces of shea butter oil
- 23 ounces of coconut oil
- 4 ounces of soybean oil
- 23 ounces of palm oil
- 4 ounces of castor oil

Directions:

1. Add lye slowly to beer and allow it to cool to 110 degrees. The beer and lye mixture can bubble over if the beer isn't completely flat and cold.

2. Melt oils until they reach 110 degrees.

3. Mix lye mixture and oils slowly and stir continuously until the soap traces.

4. Pour the soap into the mold. Allow to cool for 18-24 hours.

5. Cut into bars. Allow soap to cure for an additional 2 weeks.

Rosemary Dill Soap

Ingredients:

- 4.4 ounces of solid lye
- 12 ounces of distilled water
- 10 ounces of palm oil
- 6 ounces of coconut oil
- 12 ounces of olive oil
- 4 ounces of sweet almond oil
- 1/2 tablespoon coffee grounds
- 1 tablespoon ground rosemary
- 1/2 tablespoon ground dill
- 1 tablespoon rosemary essential oil

Directions:

1. Add lye to distilled water and mix. Allow it to cool to 100 degrees.

2. Measure and melt oils with the exception of a half ounce of sweet almond oil which is set aside.

3. Add the essential oil to the sweet almond oil.

4. When the temperature of both lye and oil mixtures reach 100 degrees, add lye to oils

and stir continuously until it reaches a mild trace.

5. Mix in essential oil mixture and then pour into molds.

6. Allow to cool in blankets until the soap has hardened after 18-48 hours.

7. Cut into bars. Allow soap to cure for an additional 3 weeks.

Dog Washing Soap

Don't use on cats as tea tree oil is toxic to cats.

Ingredients:

- 3.54 ounces lye
- 6 ounces of olive oil
- 8 ounces of coconut oil
- 6.5 ounces of palm oil
- 1.5 ounces of castor oil
- 3 ounces of canola oil
- 8.5 ounces of water

At trace ingredients:

- 0.5 ounces of aloe vera gel

- 0.25 ounces of jojoba oil
- 0.25 ounces of lavender essential oil
- 0.125 ounces of peppermint essential oil
- 0.25 ounces of eucalyptus essential oil
- 0.125 ounces of citronella essential oil
- 0.25 ounces T50 Tocopherol
- 0.25 ounces of neem oil
- 0.125 ounces of tea tree oil
- 0.125 ounces of lemongrass essential oil
- 0.125 ounces of cedar wood essential oil

Directions:

1. Add lye to water and allow it to cool to 110 degrees.

2. Melt oils until they reach 110 degrees.

3. Add lye solution to oils and stir continuously until it reaches trace.

4. At this point add all the other ingredients. Stir in well.

5. Pour into mold and let it cool for 24 hours.

6. Cut into bars. Allow to cure for at least 3 weeks.

Lemongrass Oatmeal Soap

Ingredients:

- 7 ounces of Crisco
- 6.2 ounces of lye
- 1 cup oatmeal, ground in blender
- 30 ounces of olive oil
- 9 ounces of soybean oil
- 17.5 ounces of green tea
- 10 green tea with lemon tea bags—take tea out of bags
- 1 ounce of lemongrass essential oil

Directions:

1. Melt Crisco along with other oils until they are just melted. Let it cool to 95 degrees.

2. Add lye to tea water, stirring the whole time.

3. Let the tea water cool to 95 degrees and mix it with the oils. Stir continuously. Then blend with a stick blender until it reaches trace.

4. At trace, mix in essential oil and oatmeal, along with the tea bag contents.

5. Pour into molds. Let it sit for 24-48 hours.

6. Cut into bars. Let the bars cure for about 3 weeks.

Coffee Soap

Ingredients:
- 9.1 ounces of lye
- 26 ounces of triple strength brewed coffee, cold
- 28 ounces of olive oil
- 16 ounces of palm oil
- 16 ounces of coconut oil
- 4 ounces of cocoa butter
- 1 ounce vanilla fragrance oil

Directions:

1. Mix lye with cold coffee and allow it to cool to 110 degrees.

2. Melt cocoa butter and add all other oils until they reach 110 degrees.

3. When temperatures are equal, slowly add lye coffee solution to oil solution. Stir con-

tinuously until it reaches trace; then add vanilla fragrance.

4. Pour into mold and let cool for 24-48 hours.

5. Cut into bars and let cure for 3 weeks.

Chapter 6: Unique Types of Soap & More Recipes

So far, you have learned how to make basic bar soap—the kind people use in the bath tub, as a shampoo bar or on the dog as shampoo. Each recipe has its different types of oils and uses different fragrances, essential oils or other ingredients that add to the quality of the bar. Each involves creating a rectangular or square mold and cutting the big block into bars of soap that are then wrapped and labeled with the type of bar and usually the date the soap was made.

Perhaps you're interested in making some more interesting types of soaps? The soaps many gourmet soap stores have are fun, unique and make bath time playful. There are also many types of liquid soaps you can learn how to make. Let's find some fun recipes:

Basic Bath Bomb

Like regular soap, this is made in two halves. The first half is the dry ingredients which are weighed out on a scale:

- 8 ounces of baking soda
- 4 ounces of citric acid
- 4 ounces of corn starch
- 4 ounces of mineral salts

The second half is the wet ingredients:

- 0.75 tablespoons water
- 2 tsp ginger peach fragrance oil (or fragrance of your choice)
- 2.5 tablespoons of light vegetable oil
- 1-2 drops of food coloring

Directions:

1. Use a large bowl to put all the dry ingredients together. Use a glass bowl because it doesn't react with anything.

2. Use a pestle or whisk to get out any clumps. Then blend the wet ingredients together in a small jar that you shake up.

3. While whisking, slowly add the wet ingredients to the dry ingredients. If you get a

foaming action, pour more slowly and whisk faster to stop the overreaction.

4. Add only about a teaspoon at a time until you get something the consistency of wet sand.

5. Use round molds or even Christmas balls designed to be filled with something. Pack the material in the mold and then pop it out onto a piece of freezer paper to dry.

6. Continue packing molds until all the mixture has been made into balls. This recipe should make about four balls. Pack the balls tightly so they don't fall apart. You can also pack ice cube trays, candy molds or even muffin tins.

7. Once dry, store bombs in an air tight bag or container. They will reactivate when placed in humid conditions. Bath bombs should be used within 6 months of making them unless you use a preservative.

Massage Oil Bath Bomb

Ingredients:

- 1 cup citric acid
- 2 cups baking soda
- 4 tsp massage oil—you can also use 2 tsp of essential oil and 2 tsp of olive oil
- Water in a spray bottle
- Two part plastic ball for mold

Directions:

1. Mix dry ingredients together and then slowly add oils.

2. Spritz with spray bottle until the mixture is the consistency of wet sand.

3. Use the two part mold to tightly pack the ball molds. This recipe makes 5 bath bombs.

4. Allow the bombs to dry out thoroughly before packaging in airtight packages.

Water Softening Bath Bomb

Ingredients:

- 1/2 cup citric acid
- 1/2 cup corn starch
- 1 cup baking soda
- 3/4 tablespoons water
- 2.5 tablespoons mixed grape seed and almond oil
- 1/2 tsp Borax
- 2 tsp fragrance oil
- Spray bottle with witch hazel in it

Directions:

1. Mix well the citric acid, corn starch, and baking soda.

2. In a separate container, mix water, cooking oil, borax, and fragrance oil.

3. Drizzle these wet ingredients into the dry ingredients to get the mixture to the texture of wet sand.

4. Press tightly into molds.

5. When they can be removed from the molds, tip out and spray the surface with

witch hazel spray. Then allow the bombs to dry out.

Moisturizing Fizzy Bombs

Ingredients:

- 1/2 cup corn starch
- 1 cup baking soda
- 1/4 cup Epsom salts
- 1/2 cup citric acid
- 0.75 tablespoons water
- 2.75 tablespoons almond oil
- 1.5 tsp essential oil or fragrance oil
- Colorant—few drops

Directions:

1. In a small bowl or cup, mix wet ingredients.

2. Mix dry ingredients really well in a large bowl. Trickle in the wet ingredients while stirring rapidly until it feels like compacted wet sand.

3. Press mix into mold and then tip out. Allow molded items to dry.

Bathtub Tints

Ingredients:

- 2 cups corn starch
- 3 cups baking soda
- 1.5 cups citric acid
- 3/4 tsp fragrance oil
- Drop or two of water soluble dye

Directions:

Mix all ingredients together and then seal them in a decorative, tied bag. The mixture will appear white until added to bath water. Use about a fourth to a half cup per tubful of water.

Milk-based Bath Bombs

Ingredients:

- 1/2 cup finely ground Epsom salts
- 1/4 cup powdered milk
- 1/2 cup corn starch
- 1 cup baking soda
- 1/2 cup citric acid
- 3-7 tsp of a blend of distilled water and witch hazel (1:1) in spray bottle

- 2 tablespoons olive oil infused with Calendula petals
- 2 tsp melted cocoa butter
- 1 tsp essential oil or fragrance

Directions:

1. Mix all dry ingredients well.

2. Drizzle a combination of the olive oil, melted butter and fragrance over the dry mix, mixing with your hands.

3. Use witch hazel blend in a spray bottle and spray until the mixture is the consistency of wet sand.

4. Pack tightly into molds and then turn out. Allow bath bombs to dry.

Cupcake Bath Bombs

Ingredients:

- 2 cups baking soda
- 1 cup citric acid
- 5 drops fragrance
- 1 tablespoon essential oil
- 3-5 drops colorant

- Witch hazel in a spray bottle
- Silicone cupcake molds (to place the cupcake liner in)
- 1 tsp Bentonite clay (optional)
- 1 tsp to 1 tbsp of sodium lauryl sulfate (optional)
- Paper cupcake liners

Directions:

1. Put all dried ingredients in a bowl and gently mix them thoroughly.

2. Add fragrance to the dry ingredients and mix.

3. Knead the dry ingredients as you spray with witch hazel. Mix until dry mixture is the consistency of wet sand.

4. Quickly pack them into liners and make sure you pack them in tightly. Allow them to set in silicone mold for 5-10 minutes before removing.

5. Add frosting (see below).

Frosting ingredients:

- 1 pound powdered sugar by weight

- 3 tablespoons meringue powder or powdered egg whites
- 5-6 tablespoons warm water
- 1/4 tsp Cream of Tartar
- Few drops colorant
- Few drops of colorant

Directions:

1. Mix meringue powder into warm water in a glass bowl.

2. Add cream of tartar and powdered sugar.

3. Beat with mixer on high. Add extra water if too thick. Beat for up to 9 minutes.

4. Add colorant and fragrance and mix further.

5. Spoon into a disposable cake frosting bag and pipe onto the cupcakes.

6. Allow the frosting to harden. Package in little cellophane bags and tie.

Basic Liquid Hand Soap

This takes longer and is more difficult to make right than regular soap but a good batch will last you a long time:

Ingredients:

- 7 ounces castor oil
- 10 ounces olive oil
- 2 ounces avocado oil
- 9 ounces sunflower oil
- 18 ounces coconut oil
- 4 ounces cocoa butter
- 10.7 ounces potassium hydroxide flakes
- 36 ounces distilled water

Directions:

1. Make a double boiler and bring water to a gentle boil.

2. Melt butters and oils to around 160 degrees.

3. Mix lye and water and stir until clear.

4. Add lye water to oil as soon as possible after it forms a solution. Stir until trace,

which is about as thick as Elmer's glue or a bit thicker.

5. Cover the double boiler and, after 10 minutes, remove the soap pot and mix in double boiler if it has begun to separate.

6. Remove soap pot every thirty minutes or so and stir for about three hours total or more.

7. The soap will gradually come to be more translucent. It becomes thicker as you stir, similar to a paste. When you have a translucent globe of paste, you are ready to go on.

8. In a second pot, boil 6 pounds 2 ounces of distilled water, adding 3 tablespoons of Borax to the water. Now add the glob/paste to the water and mix.

9. Add a tablespoon and a half of preservative (Germaben II, Germall Plus or GSE) and add 1/4 cup of liquid glycerin. Stir together and let sit for a few days.

10. The paste mixture should be stirred a few times a day to ensure that paste gets dissolved. After about 4 days, there will be a

thin white layer on the top which gets skimmed off. Color and scent while warming the mixture will make a nice liquid soap. Some essential oils and fragrance oils will cloud up your liquid soap.

Coconut Oil Soap

Ingredients:

- 14 ounces potassium hydroxide
- 48 ounces of coconut oil
- 42 ounces of distilled water

Directions:

1. Warm coconut oil in double boiler to 160 degrees.

2. Mix potassium hydroxide in distilled water and add oil to lye solution stirring until mixed.

3. Heat for 30 minutes before stirring again.

4. Repeat this until 4 hours have past and until you have a translucent glob in the bottom of the pan.

Other choices include a mild coconut recipe:

- 13 ounces of potassium hydroxide
- 35 ounces coconut oil
- 13 ounces of olive oil
- 39 ounces of distilled water

Also, you can make cold cream soap:

- 13 ounces of potassium hydroxide
- 35 ounces of coconut
- 3 ounces palm oil
- 11 ounces of castor oil
- 30 ounces of water

In all cases, you melt the solid oils and then add the liquid oils. You stir in your lye and water mixture. You can use a stick blender to make a blob faster. Stir once or twice a day for three days. Then dilute and neutralize your soap. Add between 9 ounces to 48 ounces of water to a pound of paste, depending on how thin or thick you want your soap. Allow it to gradually mix together over several days, stirring a couple of times per day at room temperature.

The following things can neutralize diluted soap:

- Citric acid

- Boric acid
- Borax

Add two ounces of any of the above to 8 ounces of boiling water until dissolved. Then mix with soap. Soap can then be bottled and cured for up to 6 months.

Jojoba Liquid Soap

Ingredients:

- 2 ounces jojoba oil
- 8.9 ounces of potassium hydroxide
- 10 ounces of castor oil
- 18 ounces of coconut oil
- 10 ounces of sunflower oil
- 26.7 ounces distilled water
- 4 tablespoons of 5 percent borax solution per 8 ounces of soap paste
- 0.3 ounces of essential oil or fragrance per 8 ounces of soap paste
- 8 ounces of distilled water per 8 ounces of soap paste.

Directions:

1. Melt oils and, in a separate pot, mix lye and water.

2. Mix the lye and oil together and bring to trace.

3. Cook paste for 4.5 hours, stirring every 30 minutes. Jojoba oil is opaque so you won't have a translucent paste.

4. Neutralize with a 5 percent Borax solution (0.5 ounces of Borax in 9.5 ounces near boiling water). It will take about 4 tablespoons to neutralize the soap.

5. Add about 9-10 ounces of water per 8 ounces of paste.

6. Add colorant and fragrance.

7. Allow the paste to dissolve in the water (up to a week). Stir a couple of times per day. Pour into bottles and use.

Foam Soap

This is the soap that foams when you put it in a foam soap container that you can get in bulk at online soap making stores. All recipes include Castile liquid soap, which is made as follows:

Ingredients:

- 1 cup grated Castile soap, firmly packed
- 2 tablespoons vegetable glycerin
- 4 cups water

Directions:

Mix these together and use a stick blender to blend into a smooth liquid soap. You may have to slightly heat the water and soap mixture to get it blended in.

Pine Blend Foam Soap

You'll need an 8 ounce foam soap container

Ingredients:

- 7 ounces of liquid Castile soap
- 25 drops Sweet Orange essential oil
- 30 drops of Hemlock essential oil
- 25 drops Siberian Fir essential oil

Directions:

Mix these together in a container and pour into foam soap container.

Citrus Sunshine Foam Soap

Ingredients:

- 8 ounce foam soap container
- 7 ounces of liquid Castile soap
- 20 drops steam distilled lime essential oil
- 30 drops of grapefruit essential oil
- 25 drops sweet orange essential oil

Directions:

Mix these together in a container and add to foam soap container.

Germ Fighting Foam Soap

Ingredients:

- 8 ounce foam soap container
- 7 ounces of liquid Castile soap
- 30 drops lavender essential oil
- 15 drops Palmarosa essential oil
- 30 drops tea tree essential oil
- 20 drops Thyme CT linalol essential oil

Directions:

Mix together in a container and serve up in an 8 ounce foam container.

Sweet Foam Soap

Ingredients:

- 8 ounce foam soap container
- 7 ounce liquid Castile soap
- 30 drops sweet orange essential oil
- 40 drops cardamom CO2 extract
- 10 drops steam distilled lime essential oil

Directions:

Mix together and put into 8 ounce foam soap container.

Shampoo Recipes

There are many different kinds of shampoos you can make yourself. Some have a long shelf life, while others need to be refrigerated to keep in good condition.

Basic Shampoo

Ingredients:

- 1/2 tsp jojoba oil or grapeseed oil
- 1/4 cup liquid Castile soap
- 1/4 cup distilled water

Directions:

Mix all ingredients together and store in a shampoo bottle. Shake vigorously before use. It only takes a little bit to lather your whole head.

Stimulant Shampoo

This is a very refreshing shampoo for all hair types.

Ingredients:

- 1/4 cup liquid Castile soap
- 2 tsp jojoba oil
- 1/4 cup water
- 1/2 tsp tea tree essential oil
- 1/2 tsp peppermint essential oil

Directions:

Mix all ingredients and then add 1/4 cup of distilled water. Use like regular shampoo.

Dry Hair Shampoo

This is a good shampoo for dry hair.

Ingredients:

- 1/4 cup liquid Castile soap
- 1/4 cup distilled water
- 1/4 tsp avocado oil or jojoba oil
- 1/4 cup aloe vera gel
- 1 tsp glycerin

Directions:

Mix all ingredients together. Use like regular shampoo. Shake well before use.

Chamomile Tea Shampoo

This is considered a calming shampoo. Combine this shampoo with lemon juice to naturally lighten your hair.

Ingredients:

- 1 cup Castile soap
- 1 cup distilled water
- 1.5 tbsp glycerin
- 6 chamomile tea bags

Directions:

1. Steep the tea bags in a cup of boiling distilled water for 20 minutes. Remove and discard the tea bags.

2. Add Castile soap to the tea mixture.

3. Add glycerin and use. Store in a dark cool location in a bottle you can seal.

Antidandruff Shampoo

This is especially good for those who have dandruff.

Ingredients:

- 1/4 cup liquid Castile soap
- 1/4 cup distilled water
- 3 tablespoon apple juice
- 1/2 tsp grapeseed oil, jojoba oil or other light vegetable oil
- 1 tablespoon apple cider vinegar
- 6 completely ground cloves

Directions:

1. Using a blender, mix all ingredients for about 30 seconds.

2. Cover and refrigerate leftovers. This product lasts only three days.

Shiny Hair Shampoo

Ingredients:

- 1/4 cup liquid Castile soap
- 1/4 cup distilled water
- 1/4 tsp lemon essential oil
- 2 tablespoons dried rosemary
- 2 tablespoons sweet almond oil

Directions:

1. Boil distilled water and add rosemary to steep for several minutes.

2. Strain out leaves and cool mixture.

3. Mix in the rest of the ingredients and store in a sealed bottle. Use like you would any shampoo.

Rejuvenating Shampoo

Ingredients:

- 1/4 cup liquid Castile soap
- 1/4 cup distilled water
- 1/2 tsp vanilla extract
- 1/2 tsp jojoba or grapeseed oil

- 3 tablespoons rosemary
- 2 tsp tea tree oil
- 1 tablespoon lemongrass

Directions:

1. Boil distilled water and add lemongrass and rosemary.

2. Steep for about 30 minutes. Strain out leaves and cool tea.

3. Add the rest of the ingredients, stirring well, adding the tea tree oil and vanilla last.

4. When mixed, you store the shampoo in a bottle and use like any other shampoo.

Coconut Shampoo

Ingredients:
- 1/4 cup liquid Castile soap
- 10 drops vanilla fragrance oil
- 2 tsp jojoba
- 10 drops coconut fragrance oil

Directions:

Just mix all the ingredients together and store in a bottle. It smells good enough to drink.

In Between Hair Treatment

This is an unusual treatment for those in between times when you can't shampoo or for camping when you don't have water.

Ingredients:

- 1 tsp crushed lavender
- 1 tsp baking soda
- 1/4 cup dry oatmeal

Directions:

1. Grind the mixture together with a mortar and pestle and place in a baggie.

2. Take some out and sprinkle over hair.

3. Rub it in the hair and then brush the particulate matter out.

4. Store in a cool and dry place.

No Frills Shampoo

Ingredients:

- 1 cup liquid Castile soap
- 1/4 cup water
- 2 tablespoons apple cider vinegar
- 3/4 tablespoon tea tree oil

Directions:

Mix all ingredients & place in a 16-ounce spray bottle.

Laundry Detergent Recipes

There are several kinds of laundry detergents you can make and use for pennies a load. They clean just about any kind of laundry.

Detergent One

Ingredients:

- 2 cups grated bar soap
- 1 qt boiling water
- 2 cups washing soda
- 2 cups Borax

Directions:

1. Add the finely grated bar soap to boiling water, stirring until soap is melted.

2. Keep mixture on low heat until it is completely melted.

3. Pour soapy water into a large pail and add the borax and washing soda.

4. Add 2 gallons water and stir until completely mixed.

5. For each laundry load, stir liquid well and use 1/4 cup per load.

Detergent Two

Ingredients:

- 1 grated bar of soap
- 1/2 cup Borax
- 1 pint hot water
- 1 cup washing soda

Directions:

1. Add grated bar to water and stir over medium heat until soap is melted.

2. Fill a ten gallon jug half full of steaming water.

3. Add the soap mixture, washing soda and Borax and stir until all powder is completely dissolved.

4. Fill the pail with more hot water.

5. When washing clothing, use a cup per load, stirring soap before each use because the soap will form a gel.

Detergent Three

Ingredients:

- 3 pints hot water
- 1/3 grated bar of soap
- 1/2 cup Borax
- 1/2 cup washing soda

Directions:

1. Heat up three pints of water and add grated bar, stirring until melted.

2. Add the Borax and washing soda until all powder is dissolved.

3. Remove solution from heat.

4. Take a 2 gallon pail and pour the heated mixture and another quart of hot water.

5. Fill rest of pail with cold water, stirring everything well.

6. When cleaning laundry, use a half cup per load, stirring the pail because it will get.

Detergent Four

This is a powdered recipe for those who like powdered laundry detergent.

Ingredients:

- 2 cups Fels Naphtha Soap, finely grated
- 1 cup washing soda
- 1 cup Borax

Directions:

Mix the dry mixture together well and store in an airtight plastic container. For each load, use 2 tablespoons of the mixture.

Detergent Five

Ingredients:

- 1 bar ivory soap, grated
- 2.5 gallons of hot water
- 1 cup of washing soda

Directions:

1. Melt grated soap with about a pint of water, heated over low to medium heat.

2. Fill large bucket with 2.5 gallons hot water.

3. Add soap mixture and stir well.

4. Add washing soda and stir it in until dissolved. Allow to cool.

5. Use a half cup of the mixture per load. Stir carefully before taking a half cup out.

Detergent Six

Ingredients:

- 1 bar grated soap
- 2.5 gallons hot water
- 2 tablespoons glycerin
- 3/4 cup Borax
- 3/4 cup washing soda

Directions:

1. Melt grated soap within a small amount of water.

2. Take a large bucket and pour 2.5 gallons hot water.

3. Add melted mixture, Borax, glycerin and washing soda. Mix until dissolved.

4. When washing, use a half cup per load.

Detergent Seven

Ingredients:

- 2 cups grated bar soap
- 2.5 gallons hot water
- 2 cups washing soda

Directions:

1. Melt bar soap with an amount of water to cover soap.

2. Heat and stir until dissolved.

3. Pour 2.5 gallons of water into large bucket and add soap mixture.

4. Add washing soda and stir until dissolved. Use a cupful per wash load.

Detergent Eight

Ingredients:

- 1 grated bar of soap
- 2 gallons hot water
- 2 cups baking soda

Directions:

1. Melt grated soap in an amount of water to cover.

2. Cook the mixture over medium low heat until soap is melted.

3. Take a large bucket to which you add 2 gallons of hot water.

4. Add melted soap and baking soda.

5. Use one half cup per regular load or one cup for very dirty loads.

Detergent Nine

Ingredients:

- 8 cups grated bar soap
- 8 cups washing soda
- 8 cups baking soda
- 12 cups Borax

Directions:

Mix all ingredients together and seal in a tub. Use 1/8 of the powder for each load.

Detergent Ten

Ingredients:

- 1/4 cup liquid Castile soap
- 1 cup baking soda
- 1 cup washing soda
- 1 cup white vinegar

Directions:

1. Pour Castile soap into bowl and stir in the washing soda.

2. Stir in the baking soda and finally add the vinegar in small amounts at a time.

3. Break down lumps and use a half cup per full load.

Chapter 7: Starting a Soap Making Business

If you really like soap making and have decided to open a soap making business, you have to make some decisions. What kinds of products will you sell? Where will you make the soap? What additional products to you need to buy? Where will you sell the product and how will you market it? How much should I charge? These are questions you must answer before you start your business.

What kinds of products will you sell? Some soap companies just make bar soap. Others extend themselves to liquid hand soap or great gifts like bath bombs and cupcake bath bombs. These sell well and are great products to include in your collection. Some items will need preservatives in order to have a long enough shelf life.

Where will you make the soap? There is no reason you can't continue to make your soap in your kitchen or in your basement. Set up a little work shop so that you have soaps curing while molds are solidifying and being cut. That way you can be at different stages along the way to making several different types of soap at once.

You may need to get some new equipment. You'll need more molds and you'll need to find a way to package your soaps, which may involve a large roll of saran wrap and a large sticker with your name and the name of the soap on it. You'll need to create a catchy name for your soap brand.

Where will you sell the product and how will you market it? You'll have to have a web site that lists your products and that may or may not have the ability to help you sell soap online. You could also have your own soap boutique at the local mall or put your soaps into boutique stores to be sold outright or on consignment. Craft fairs and bazaars are great places to sell your wares.

How much should you charge? You need to determine how much it costs per bar to make. Then you need to mark up the bar cost by about 200-300 percent if you're selling them at a boutique or online. You'll need to consider your market before deciding how much to sell your bars for. Some markets will allow you to sell your bars for more money.

In order to be good at soap making, you need to spend some time practicing the art. This means making different recipes several times over and testing your product to make sure it looks good, smells good and works the way it is supposed to. Try your soap making out in different conditions and make sure each batch turns out the same. Study the science of soap making so you recognize the different ways lye mixes with oils or fats to produce a variety of kinds of soap.

Start by renting some space at a local festival or craft fair. You can sell hundreds of bars of soap in just one weekend which will give you seed money for the purposes of making more bars of soap. Make a little catalogue or brochure to give out with each sale. Then you can expect some repeat customers through your website or through your store front.

Just make soap and don't worry about the details of whether or not you will be able to make soap and sell it. This should be a labor of love that you do for the joy of making soap; the selling of soap should just naturally come out of the joy you feel when the mold pops out. Making beautiful soap should be the goal;

people will buy really beautiful soap and it takes practice to be able to do this right.

Invest in some professional molds so you can make perfect bars of soap. When you're making soap for profit, the mold and the bars should look nearly perfect. It doesn't look so good to have odd shaped bars wrapped for sale.

Make unique bars of soap that make your soap stand out from all the rest. Make them all out of essential oils for a natural scent, make soap out of milk and make some interesting colored natural soaps. Try to set your soap apart from others who make soap. Follow your own path to making unique soap and people will buy it.

Once you've got your business set up, pay attention to the basic legal things you need to do in order to sell soap legally. If your soap business has a name, you may want to copyright the name so no one else can use your name.

Get a license to be a sole proprietor if this is required in your state. Check with a tax person to see if you should simply be a sole proprietor or a limited liability company or LLC. An LLC protects your personal assets. If you're going to be an LLC, you need to file this with the state and it will cost you at least $300 to get your business permit. You'll then get a sales tax permit for the state and a federal tax identification number from the federal government. If it's just you making and selling the soap, you can be a sole proprietor but if you have employees, you may just want to be an LLC.

You'll want to have insurance to protect your business assets in case one of your products causes an injury or damage to a client. It also protects you from business loss due to theft or fire. For a soap making business, your products are low cost and you should be able to get business insurance for around $600 to $1000 per year. Your property insurance may also cover your business items.

You'll want to figure out how much your supplies cost, including your stick blender, mold costs and the cost of all the oils, fragrances, lye, and essential oils. It will cost you about $150 to about $500 to get started so you'll want to recoup those costs in the first few batches of bars. Get as much as you can wholesale because you'll get larger quantities at a reduced price.

Get educated in making soap by attending a soap making class or doing online tutorials related to the making of soap. Get new recipes and project ideas; learn about the latest in products used to make soap. There are forums for making soap in which new ideas are shared.

As mentioned, you need a website. This costs about $20 per month or use a craft site like Etsy or Dawanda, which are marketplaces for people who are selling handmade items. You need to know something about creating a website but, if you are opening a store that actually sells items to customers on the web, you may need the expertise of someone who makes these kinds of websites for a living and who can help you update the site when new products come online.

You may need to advertise your product. Why not target your advertising to pet stores if you sell dog washing products or to hotels for custom products in their guest rooms? You should be able to get a few of these places to agree to stock your line of specialized soaps to their customers. This could mean you're making lots of product at a time but what's better than that? Make a brochure with your company name, pictures and descriptions of your best soaps, and your contact information. This could turn out to be big business for you.

This isn't to say that starting and maintaining a soap making business won't be challenging but if you enjoy creativity and the art of making soap, it should be fun and profitable for you.

Chapter 8: Putting it All Together

As you have learned, making soap has a long history and tradition. Many people made soap by chance and others painstakingly learned the craft through trial and error. Even with the many recipes provided, your journey into soap making will involve some trial and error. Even when you think you have everything perfectly measured out, there can be something in the environment or something in the way the ingredients are mixed that causes a batch to come out imperfectly.

Try the recipes and find those that suit you. Then experiment on your own. You can make hundreds of kinds of bar soap as well as liquid soap, bath bombs, foamy soaps and even laundry soaps. Each has a slightly different technique to learn and to master. Start with whatever technique appeals to you and then try others. You can make soaps that are soothing, exfoliating or just plain smell good.

In this guide, you learned to work with sodium hydroxide, which makes hard soap, and potassium hydroxide, which makes liquid soap. Both are highly caustic agents that shouldn't be touched without rubber gloves. Wear eye protection because lye in your eye can cause permanent caustic damage to the eyes. You should also not touch raw soap that hasn't solidified. Curing the soap takes out some of the alkalinity so the soap is gentler to the touch and feels better on your skin.

You also learned about the qualities of different oils. Some create softer soaps, while others tend to make hard soap. No soap has just one type of oil in it (although it technically could) so the soaps all have qualities of each kind of oil in it. Follow the recipes and you should do fine.

Making soap can be something you just do for fun or you can do it for profit. If you start a soap making business, you'll probably need a log of which soaps you've made and when you made them so you can keep track of curing times and the times you can safely cut the soap into bars.

Set up a website and make brochures, prepared for customers. Try renting out space at a craft fair or bazaar and see how well your soap sells. In some cases, packaging is everything. Package your soaps so the customer can smell the soap inside and has a sticker to take home that allows them the opportunity to buy more bars because it has your identifying information and website on the package.

Most of all, enjoy making soap. It is a time honored practice that has found a new niche among people who want natural soaps to use at bath time.

Made in the USA
Columbia, SC
23 March 2019